Titles in this series
Don't Call Me Special - a first look at disability
I Can Be Safe - a first look at safety
I Miss You - a first look at death
Is it Right to Fight? - a first look at conflict
My Parents Picked Me! - a first look at adoption
Stop Picking on Me - a first look at bullying
The Skin I'm In - a first look at racism

Text copyright © Pat Thomas 2001
Illustrations copyright © Lesley Harker 2001

Editor: Liz Gogerly
Consultant: Nick Tapp, East Sussex Disability Association
Concept design: Kate Buxton
Design: Jean Wheeler

Published in Great Britain by Hodder Wayland,
an imprint of Hodder Children's Books
This edition Published in 2005

Reprinted in 2006, 2007, 2008 and 2010

British Library Cataloguing in Publication Data

Thomas, Pat, 1959-
  First look at disability
  1.Handicapped
  I.Title II.Harker, Lesley III.Disability
  362.4

  ISBN: 978-0-3409-1107-5

Printed in China

Wayland
338 Euston Road
London NW1 3BH

Wayland is an imprint of Hachette Children's
Books, an Hachette UK Company.
www.hachette.co.uk

Don't Call Me Special

A FIRST LOOK AT DISABILITY

PAT THOMAS
ILLUSTRATED BY LESLEY HARKER

WAYLAND

Some children find it really hard to join in with sports and games in the playground.

You probably picked out the girl in the wheelchair.
Lots of people would guess that because
she is disabled she wouldn't be
interested in sports.

Actually it's this boy.

He hates sports because he can't run as fast as his friends and he always gets pushed around.

Sometimes when we see people who are different from us we assume things about them that are not always true.

When you assume, you are just making a guess. Assuming things about people can hurt their feelings and make them feel very left out.

Everybody in the world is unique. That means that each one of us is a little different from everyone else.

We each have things that we can do easily, and things that we find hard and need help with.

What about you?

Do you know any disabled children in your school? In your family?
What things are they good at? What do they find difficult? What are you
good at? What do you find difficult?

If you need glasses to see or special scissors to cut with, you are using special equipment to help you do your best.

What about you?

What kinds of disability do you know about? Can you think of some types of equipment (like glasses to help a person see) that help disabled people.

Disabled children often use helpful equipment too. They use ramps to make getting from one place to another easier. They have special toilets and sinks or special types of mouse and keyboards to help them use the computer.

Some children are born disabled and
some are disabled because they
have had an illness or been
in an accident.

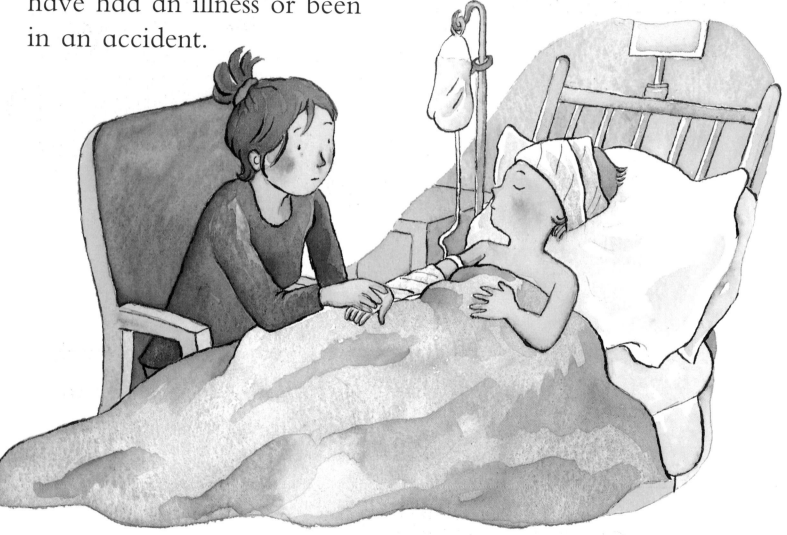

There are many different types of disability. There are some where parts of your body don't work so well.

There are some which make it hard to learn as fast as others.

Years ago disabled children went to special schools with special teachers. Because of this people started calling them 'special'.

18

Today many disabled people dislike being called special because it makes them sound too different from everyone else.

19

Now many disabled children go to ordinary schools.
That's because we know that the world is more
interesting when we can all be together
and learn from each other.

And even though
a disabled child may
sometimes look different on
the outside, inside they are just like you.

They feel angry and sad when they are teased and they feel happy and confident when they are loved.

Some disabled children have extra teachers or helpers who work with them at school and at home. Sometimes these helpers are adults and sometimes they are children in the class.

A helper's job is just to help.
It can be very upsetting
when a helper tries to
do everything.

No two people learn things in the
same way or at the same speed.

Some disabled children take longer
to do or learn things, or they do
them in a different way.

But sometimes they
can do things better
and learn things faster
than others.

We all need to work
and play together.

And with a little extra help disabled children can learn and grow and do the things they want to – just like everybody else.

HOW TO USE THIS BOOK

This book is an introduction to the subject of disability for young children. The information a child needs to know, or can absorb about disability, varies from child to child and sometimes depends on the age of the child. In this age group it is important to foster acceptance and tolerance of people who are in some way 'different'. The whys about disability may be more appropriately addressed by older children.

Sometimes adults need to sort out their own feelings about disability before talking to their children about it. It is only in recent years that we have begun to accept that disability does not need to be kept behind closed doors. Take some time to think through the issues before you talk to your child.

Group discussions about disability with young children are often very lively. One way to help children understand what it is like to be disabled is through play acting. A parent or teacher could help a child understand what it is like to be without one of their senses, for instance, by blindfolding them, or asking them to cover their ears. In schools where equipment is available, giving able-bodied children the opportunity to use a wheelchair or other aids may enhance their understanding of some of the difficulties faced by the disabled.

Having made it more difficult for them to see, hear or walk, this is also a good time to talk about people who have overcome disability, and even achieved greatness – such as Helen Keller, Beethoven and Christy Brown.

Schools which are attended by a diversity of children must devise a variety of ways to help the less able. These may include ramps for wheelchairs but also special scissors, paper and pencils, adapted keyboards for computers (as well as different types of mouse) and special tables and chairs. Discussions aimed at demystifying this special equipment are important because they help us see the person and not the disability. They also foster creative problem solving. Get your child to talk about the different equipment disabled people use, perhaps as part of a wider discussion about the equipment others use to help them – a special stool in the bathroom, for example.

The language we use with regard to disabled people has come a long way, but many disabled children still get labelled, called names and teased. Help your child to understand that name-calling (e.g. 'cripple' or 'idiot') is never acceptable. Likewise, help your child to use the right words to describe particular disabilities; words like 'handicapped', 'retarded' or 'spastic' are now seen as hurtful and insulting.

Giving children responsibilities is a good way to learn. If there is a disabled child in the class, make sure able-bodied students have an opportunity to be helpers.

Disability charities and self-help groups are often willing to come and talk to classes. These can be very useful. A talk on sign language or lip reading for instance, can widen children's horizons about listening and communication.

GLOSSARY

Assume When we assume something, we are making a guess without really knowing anything.

Equipment The things that we use to make some of the jobs we have to do easier.

Unique If something is unique, it is the only one of its kind. All people are unique because we are all different from each other. The things which make us unique, make us special.

RECOMMENDED READING

I'm Special
by Jen Green/Mike Gordon (Hodder Wayland, 1999)

My Brother is Different
by Louise Gorrod/Beccy Carver (National Autistic Society, 2003)

Seal Surfer
by Michael Foreman (Red Fox, 1998)

You Are Very Special
by Su Box/Susie Poole (Lion Publishing, 2000)

CONTACTS

The Alliance for Inclusive Education
Unit 2, 70 South Lambeth Road
London   SW8 1RL
020 7735 5277

British Council of Organizations of Disabled People (BCODP)
Litchurch Plaza
Litchurch Lane
Derby   DE24 8AA
01332 295551

Barnardos
Tanners Lane
Barkingside
Essex   IG6 1QG
020 8550 8822

British Institute of Learning Disabilities (BILD)
Campion House
Green Street
Kidderminster
Worcestershire   DY10 1JL
01562 723 010

Disability Information Trust
Nuffield Orthopaedic Centre
Headington
Oxford
OX3 7LD
01865 227592

Council for Disabled Children
National Children's Bureau
8 Wakley Street
London   EC1V 7QE
020 7843 1900